SCENE BY SCENE COMPARATIVE WORKBOOKS

A Doll's House
by Henrik Ibsen

Social Setting

Relationships

Hero, Heroine, Villain

Copyright © 2015 by Amy Farrell.

All rights reserved. No part of this publication may be reproduced, distributed or transmitted in any form or by any means, including photocopying, recording, or other electronic or mechanical methods, without the prior written permission of the publisher, except in the case of brief quotations embodied in critical reviews and certain other noncommercial uses permitted by copyright law. For permission requests, write to the publisher, addressed "Attention: Permissions Coordinator," at the address below.

Scene by Scene
11 Millfield, Enniskerry
Wicklow, Ireland.
www.scenebysceneguides.com

orders@scenebyscene.ie

A Doll's House Comparative Workbook OL16 by Amy Farrell. —1st ed.
ISBN 978-1-910949-08-5

2016 Ordinary Level Comparative Workbook

'A Doll's House' by Henrik Ibsen

The modes at Ordinary Level for 2016 are:

Social Setting

This mode refers to the setting and social world of the text.

Consider the roles of men and women, race, religion, social class, etc.

Relationships

This mode refers to the relationships between characters in the story.

Consider whether relationships are difficult, if they make characters happy or unhappy, their importance in the story, etc.

Hero, Heroine, Villain

This mode refers to the study and analysis of a specific lead character.

Consider the character's personality, behavior, what you like and dislike about them, etc.

About This Workbook

Our workbooks are for the Leaving Certificate Comparative Study.

Each workbook is divided into three coloured sections, one for each comparative mode. This makes it easy to identify each mode and make comparisons and contrasts between texts – simply use matching coloured sections of each of your workbooks to identify similarities and differences.

Each coloured section has two parts to it. The first part focuses on the text itself, and asks text-specific questions within a comparative mode. This helps you get familiar with the text and the aspects of the text that are covered by that mode.

The second part of each section focuses on one of the modes. In this part, you are asked more general, mode-specific questions. You then have to take what you know about the text and apply it to the mode. By doing this you will become very familiar with what each mode involves, and it will help prepare you for writing comparative answers.

Once complete, this workbook will become your set of notes, to revise and study before the exam, and to help you when preparing comparative essays for class.

We hope our workbooks help you conquer the comparative!

Best wishes,

The team at Scene by Scene

scenebysceneguides.com

A Doll's House by Henrik Ibsen
Social Setting

A DOLL'S HOUSE - SOCIAL SETTING

Where does the story take place? Describe the house where the action takes place. Use quotes/examples to support your points.

When does the story take place? Use quotes/examples to support your points.

KNOW THE TEXT

How do the people in this story make a living?

Are the Helmers rich or poor? Use quotes/examples to support your view.

A DOLL'S HOUSE - SOCIAL SETTING

What is Nora's role in the household?

Is she happy with this role?

KNOW THE TEXT

What is Torvald's role in the household?

How does Torvald treat his wife? Use quotes/examples to support your view.

A DOLL'S HOUSE - SOCIAL SETTING

Do Nora and Mrs. Linde have a good friendship?

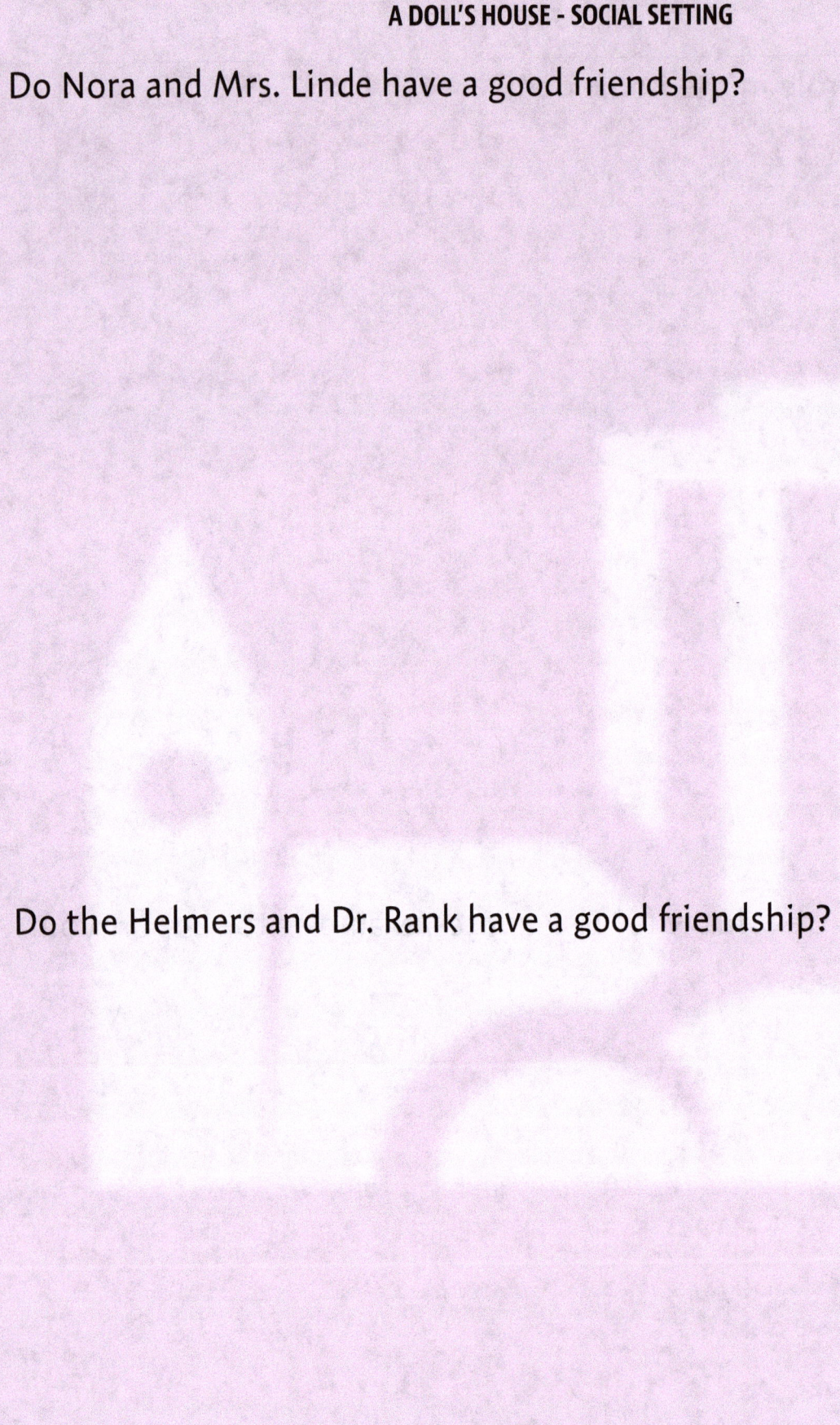

Do the Helmers and Dr. Rank have a good friendship?

KNOW THE TEXT

Do you think Mrs. Linde and Krogstad will be happy together?

What is Nora not allowed do, because she is a woman?

A DOLL'S HOUSE - SOCIAL SETTING

What is Nora's 'crime'? What does it tell you about the Social Setting?

When Torvald discovers Nora's secret, how does he react? What does this tell you about the Social Setting?

KNOW THE TEXT

What does Torvald value in life?

What does Nora value in life?

Is Nora a good mother?

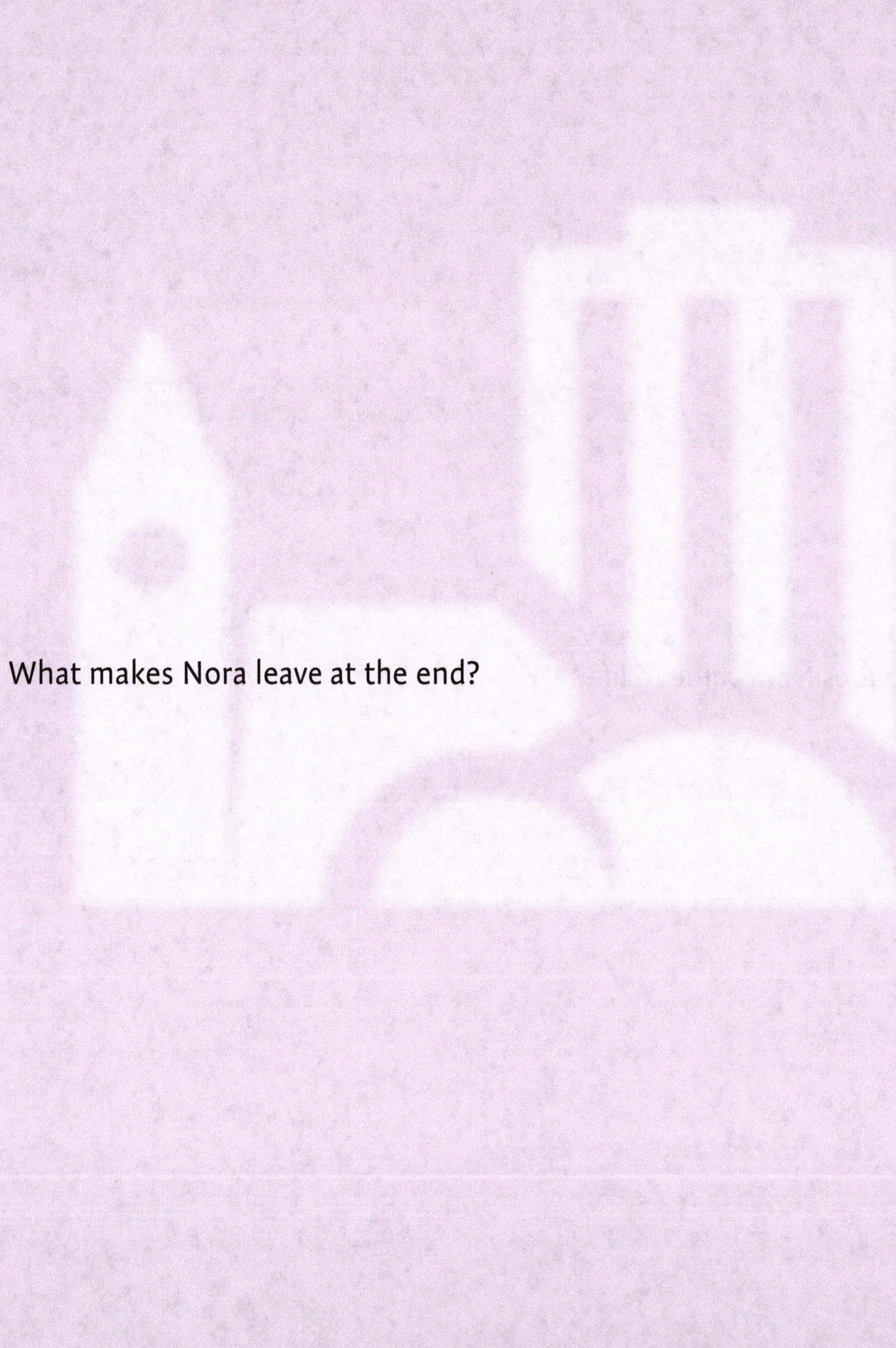

What makes Nora leave at the end?

Did she do the right thing, in your opinion?

Describe the **setting** of this text.

KNOW THE MODE

What is the **role of women** in this text?

A DOLL'S HOUSE - SOCIAL SETTING

What is the **role of men** in this story?

KNOW THE MODE

How are **children treated** in the world of this story?

A DOLL'S HOUSE - SOCIAL SETTING

Is **family** important to the characters in this story?

KNOW THE MODE

Is **religion** important to the characters in this story?

A DOLL'S HOUSE - SOCIAL SETTING

Do the characters in this story hold **traditional beliefs**?

KNOW THE MODE

Is the setting of this text a **violent** or **peaceful** place?

A DOLL'S HOUSE - SOCIAL SETTING

Is this a **secure** or **dangerous** world?

KNOW THE MODE

Where do you see **conflict** in this text?

A DOLL'S HOUSE - SOCIAL SETTING

How are **characters affected** by the Social Setting of this story?

KNOW THE MODE

Would you like to live in the world of this text? Why/why not?

KNOW THE MODE

Choose **key moments** from the play that **highlight the Social Setting** of the text.

KNOW THE MODE

A DOLL'S HOUSE - SOCIAL SETTING

What **similarities** do you notice between the Social Setting of this text and your other comparative texts?

KNOW THE MODE

A DOLL'S HOUSE - SOCIAL SETTING

What **differences** do you notice between the Social Setting of this text and your other comparative texts?

KNOW THE MODE

A DOLL'S HOUSE - SOCIAL SETTING

A Doll's House by Henrik Ibsen
Relationships

A DOLL'S HOUSE - RELATIONSHIPS

In the first two Acts, does Nora care about her husband, Torvald?

What did she do to save Torvald's life?

Why did she have to keep her actions a secret when she saved her husband's life?

KNOW THE TEXT

Is Nora a dutiful, obedient wife in the first two Acts?

How does Nora act around Torvald?

Why does she act like this around her husband?

A DOLL'S HOUSE - RELATIONSHIPS

Does Torvald care about his wife, Nora?

How does Torvald view his wife?

Is Torvald a controlling husband?

KNOW THE TEXT

Does Torvald treat Nora like a child?

When it comes to Torvald, does Nora act like a child?

Does Torvald have a realistic view of their marriage?

A DOLL'S HOUSE - RELATIONSHIPS

Does Torvald really know his wife?

Are there elements of fantasy/pretence in their marriage?

What sort of relationship did Nora have with her father?

KNOW THE TEXT

How does the title of the play refer to Nora and Torvald's relationship?

During the play, how does Nora view Torvald?

How does she view him at the end?

A DOLL'S HOUSE - RELATIONSHIPS

What brought about this change in how Nora views her marriage?

In your view, do Nora and Torvald have a good relationship?

What strengths do you see in their relationship?

KNOW THE TEXT

What weaknesses do you see in their relationship?

Does their marriage bring them happiness?

Do Nora and Mrs. Linde have a good friendship?

A DOLL'S HOUSE - RELATIONSHIPS

Does Dr. Rank have a good relationship with the Helmers?

Do Mrs. Linde and Krogstad have a good relationship?

Is Nora a good mother to her children?

KNOW THE MODE

Are relationships **generally positive** (warm, supportive, nurturing, genuine) or **negative** (cold, cruel, destructive, false) in the play?

A DOLL'S HOUSE - RELATIONSHIPS

What makes relationships in the story **difficult**?

KNOW THE MODE

What would improve relationships in the play?

A DOLL'S HOUSE - RELATIONSHIPS

How do relationships **change** during the play?

KNOW THE MODE

Does this play teach us anything about relationships?

A DOLL'S HOUSE - RELATIONSHIPS

What is the **most important** relationship in the play? What makes it so important?

KNOW THE MODE

Do relationships in the play bring characters **happiness** or **unhappiness**?

A DOLL'S HOUSE - RELATIONSHIPS

Choose **key moments** from the play that **highlight relationships** in the text.

KNOW THE MODE

KNOW THE MODE

A DOLL'S HOUSE - RELATIONSHIPS

What **similarities** do you notice in the relationships of this text and your other comparative texts?

KNOW THE MODE

55

A DOLL'S HOUSE - RELATIONSHIPS

What **differences** do you notice in the relationships of this text and your other comparative texts?

KNOW THE MODE

57

A Doll's House by Henrik Ibsen
Hero, Heroine, Villain

KNOW THE TEXT

Describe Nora, the **heroine** of this play.

What are her **strengths**? (her good/strong points)

A DOLL'S HOUSE - HERO, HEROINE, VILLAIN

What are her **weaknesses**? (her flaws/weak points)

What **problems** does she face?

KNOW THE TEXT

Does she overcome these problems? Why/why not?

Is Nora **brave** (heroic) in this story? Explain you view.

What does Nora discover about her marriage?

What does Nora discover about herself?

KNOW THE TEXT

Why does she walk out on her family at the end of the play?

Did she do the right thing, by walking out on her husband and children?

A DOLL'S HOUSE - HERO, HEROINE, VILLAIN

Do you feel sympathy for Nora? Explain your view.

Did you like Nora at the start of the play?

KNOW THE TEXT

Did you like Nora by the end of the play?

How did she change, during the course of the play?

What did you **like** about Nora, the central character?

KNOW THE MODE

What did you **dislike** about this character?

Is she an **emotional** character? Use examples to support your view.

KNOW THE MODE

What do you **admire** about the Nora?

Is this character a **heroine or villain**? Explain your choice.

KNOW THE MODE

On a scale of one to ten, with one being an extremely heroic character and ten being an evil villain, where would you place Nora? Explain your choice.

Overall, did *you* **like** this character? Explain your opinion.

KNOW THE MODE

Is this character happy or sad?

A DOLL'S HOUSE - HERO, HEROINE, VILLAIN

Would you like to meet this character?

KNOW THE MODE

If you met her, what would you talk about?

A DOLL'S HOUSE - HERO, HEROINE, VILLAIN

What advice would you give this character, if you met her?

KNOW THE MODE

Is this character, a 'good' (successful/interesting) main character?

Identify the **key moments** in the play that illustrate Nora's personality/character.

KNOW THE MODE

A DOLL'S HOUSE - HERO, HEROINE, VILLAIN

How is Nora **similar** to the Hero, Heroine, Villain in your other texts?

KNOW THE MODE

How is Nora **different** to the Hero, Heroine, Villain in your other texts?

KNOW THE MODE

www.ingramcontent.com/pod-product-compliance
Lightning Source LLC
Chambersburg PA
CBHW050715090526
44587CB00019B/3386